LO
BUSES
Then and Now

LONDON TRANSPORT AT LONDON'S SERVICE

HAMMERSMITH
WALHAM GRN CHELSEA
SLOANE SQ VICTORIA
CHARING CROSS
STRAND

11

LIVERPOOL ST STN

LYR 899

dowager, of a 'certain age', the only person at her stop, was less than amused when the bus knelt before her!

The use of doored buses in Central London is less of a plus point for the present day, although the ritual dance which took place at the Centre Point stop as us intending passengers for a 25 caught in a queue of buses advanced and then retreated as the bus edged forward with no indication to show that the driver ultimately intended to stop was quite amusing to the casual observer.

I cannot recall quite so many rides which might charitably be described as 'exhilarating'. Perhaps it is the larger size of modern vehicles coupled with a higher power/weight ratio and fewer inhibitions on the part of some drivers which gives them the ability to throw the standing passenger around so successfully. Even those occupying the outside seats do well to be wary.

An abiding memory is the sight of a three-year-old bowled most efficiently down the length of the aisle of a Volvo Citybus on the 210 as the driver demonstrated the efficiency of its braking system!

Bus shelters are one thing the old LT never really got right, apparently being designed on the principle that all rain falls perfectly vertically. Now we have Adshels with protection on one side at least — and seats even — albeit of such a width as to make one appreciate the scant support offered by the minibus. But they seem to be vandal proof.

One-way schemes have proliferated since the start of our period in line with the inexorable rise of the private car. Often these seem to utilise an unsuitable collection of back streets for one of the flows — and streets through which buses seem to scuttle with undue haste with little thought for the unfortunate passenger whose goal is the main thoroughfare. The Camden Town system exemplifies this phenomenon with stops scattered at random around the area carrying maps which are not orientated in the simplest way for those unfamiliar with the area.

Not only has traffic density intensified but driving standards seem to have declined in inverse proportion. My random survey conducted as I waited, seemingly interminably, at some major centre to try to replicate an earlier view, would award the wooden spoon for driving to Golders Green.

One-way schemes and over and under passes are the more obvious manifestations of traffic management schemes but road widening and alteration to accommodate today's traffic flows has taken place in many locations. Being possessed of some instinct for self preservation, I refrained from standing in the left-hand filter lane in order to obtain the precise angle of some original pictures. I trust readers will show forbearance. And I wish so many of the original shots had not been offside views! But all in all it was a fascinating and enjoyable experience to attempt to reproduce views of up to 50 years ago sometimes involving some entertaining minor detective work. I hope the reader derives as much enjoyment as I have had in compiling it.

Finally, I would like to express my appreciation to all the photographers whose work appears in the 'Then' views (though I do wish some of them had provided caption information!) and to Simon Forty, Stephen Morris and Peter Waller whose help and encouragement were much appreciated. Kenny Hammond kindly assisted with some early route information. I am also grateful to Penelope Craddock who managed to decipher my handwriting and I am especially grateful to my wife for pointing out that today's Holloway Road/Seven Sisters Road junction is not yesterday's Archway thus saving me from one blunder — I hope there are no more though, of course, if there are the responsibility is mine.

Right:
Metrobus M181 passes ex-BEA and ex-LT RMA49, now in the fleet of Blue Triangle and awaiting sight-seeing business, on 16 April 1994. Such was the desperate vehicle shortage faced by LT in 1975 when the first RMAs were purchased that they entered service in their basic BEA livery. Subsequently, they were used for training and staff transport duties. Author

Above:
DM1109, a crew operated Fleetline, is seen in Aldwych on 25 June 1980. Author

Left:
Yet another approach to providing London's bus services: independent BTS operates route 13 with RML vehicles leased from LT. Seen here is RML2527 on 16 April 1994. The offices in the background have been rebuilt and the road layout altered. Author

Above:
The handsome lines of the Alexander body on Volvo Ailsa VI made quite an impression when it appeared as part of the Alternative Vehicles Evaluation trials based at Stockwell garage in 1984. Other types involved were Leyland Olympians, Dennis Dominators and Mark II Metrobuses. The Dominators have been withdrawn but most of the other vehicles are still in stock. Here, VI is seen in the Strand on 28 August 1984.
K. Lane

Left:
The road layout has been altered in the intervening years and route 170 now runs no further east than Clapham Junction. Refurbished RML2710 leads two other members of the class down the Strand on 16 April 1994. Author

Right:
Was this a case of biting off more than they could chew? Boro'line Maidstone successfully tendered for route 188 in 1988. Lacking sufficient vehicles of their own they hired double-deckers from Nottingham and Ipswich. Subsequently, the operator went into liquidation and this Nottingham Atlantean No 201, pictured on 24 December 1988, carries Boro'line fleetnames and LT roundels with a somewhat superfluous bus sticker in an effort to reassure confused passengers. LT itself has borrowed buses since 1949 but this was a relatively rare occurrence. Author

Above:
This 16 April 1994 shot shows that the 188 is now operated by London Country. The route still uses second hand vehicles — this time ironically an ex-LT Titan T94, now numbered 914 after acquisition in 1993. Author

Above:
War-time bomb damage can be seen as RT777 enters Aldwych. It entered service in August 1948 and would seem to be in quite new condition, having not yet received side advertisements. It carries a restricted blind display and the roof route box is not utilised. The sign points to Temple station and the Embankment tram routes. LTE

Below:
Route 9 now terminates at Aldwych but Northern Counties-bodied Scania N112DKB S59 passes a restored background in the late afternoon of 9 January 1994 whilst operating route 26. The vehicle was one of a batch of 40 delivered in June 1992, the type having initially made its LT debut at Potters Bar in 1989.
Author

Below:
Route 67 ceased to run between Waterloo and Stoke Newington in 1958 but flights to Paris and Nice for £10 and £25 respectively, together with the early postwar livery of the bus behind, suggest an early 1950s date for this view of RTL813 passing the Law Courts. LTE

Right:
Refurbished RML2616 on route 15 on 28 March 1994. A new taxi prepares to overtake the bus. Author

Above:
Daimler D173 was one of the batch of 38 CWA6s which were prepared for the restoration of Green Line services after the war. They served routes 721 and 722 and DI73 is seen on the latter at Aldgate standing on the cobbled forecourt amongst the trolleybuses. The rear of a T-type coach is visible in the background carrying roof boards for route 723.
V. C. Jones/IAL

Left:
Aldgate, alas, is no longer the major bus centre it was, hemmed in on all sides now by modern buildings. There is more interest in the contrasting rear-end designs of Metrobus M777, Titan T986 and Alexander-bodied Leyland Olympian L334 working in parallel with the Metrobus on Route 253. The date is 12 March 1994. Author

Above:
Regent Street catches the sun but MB184 looks somewhat dowdy, which is a little surprising as this is an official AEC view. It is operating Red Arrow route 505 introduced as part of the reshaping scheme in 1968. It ran until 1976 before the number was used again in 1989 for a Waterloo–London Bridge service. AEC

Left:
Christmas decorations still adorn Regent Street on 2 January 1994 as Northern Counties' Volvo B10M VN6 operates route 88, maintaining a single-decker presence in this important street. Its Clapham Omnibus logo is one of the more successful marketing ploys adopted by LT. Author

Above:
The caption on the back of this Topical Press picture of 17 July 1942 reads 'London Transport's 2,000,000 miles a year economy plan by the withdrawal of buses doing non essential work brought about a marked speeding up of traffic in the Strand and West End after the rush hour period. Instead of running back to their suburban garages with very light loads, the buses are parked at various points till wanted again in the afternoons.' *Eleven LTs are in the nearest batch and with Parliament in the background perhaps one may be permitted to say 'the eyes have it!'.*
Ian Allan Library

Below:
The Albert Embankment now provides parking for tourist coaches, though somewhat unusually on 28 February 1994 they were all from English companies. Author

Above:
Buses shared the Embankment with trams (though in the westbound direction only) from October 1950 until the last trams ran on 5 July 1952. RT3281 looks resplendent with full blind display and as yet without advertisements as it passes Embankment station. Co-existence with the trams was not always peaceful — one of RT3281's stablemates came off worse in a collision with a tram whilst emerging from Temple Place just out of view of this picture. The bus was apparently upended and finished on its side. W. H. R. Godwin

Left:
Now in the fleet of London Coaches, which was the first part of LT to be privatised in a management buy out in June 1992, convertible open topper RM710 carries hardy customers on 9 January 1994. This part of the Embankment no longer sees ordinary LT services. Author

Above:
The caption on the back of the original reads 'A warlike atmosphere was given today to the West End of London when several heavy tanks passed through on their way to "somewhere in England".' The photograph shows a tank passing round Marble Arch and the print is annotated 'Passed by Censor 19th May 1940.' Presumably it was felt that there was little point in trying to disguise Marble Arch. Buses which feature in wartime shots of bomb damage often have their details obliterated by the censor. The vehicle on the 137 is STL1199 carrying an STL 11-type body, whilst that on the 36 is an older 'General' STL. Exhortations to save surround the Arch itself. Fox

Right:
A well laden refurbished RM2379 presents a rather more peaceful view of Marble Arch on 29 March 1994. The presentation of route information along the side of the vehicle harks back to Green Line days and before that to horse buses. Marble Arch is now surrounded by a large island. Author

Above:
XMS6 was an AEC Swift with attractive Strachans standee bodywork introduced for the initial experimental Red Arrow services in April 1966. It poses here in Park Lane for its official picture.
LTE

Above right:
9 January 1994 shows a rather more exotic vehicle occupying the same location. The nearside lane of Park Lane is now largely given over to parking for tourist coaches. Author

Right:
The LT presence is still strong in this important traffic artery and veteran RM18, fitted with an Iveco engine, passes the same spot in an offside lane.
Author

Above:
A Leeds AEC Regent returns to its birthplace to assist LT during wartime vehicle shortages. Perhaps passengers have been deterred from boarding by its unusual appearance and apparent lack of route information since there only appear to be three passengers on board. Strange, since there are only four more shopping days to Christmas on 21 December 1940. AEC

Below:
The imposing buildings above Baker Street station have seen little alteration though the porte-cochere at the station entrance has been swept away. Borehamwood Transport Services seem at pains to maintain continuity, retaining the LT fleet number and only altering the livery to a deep orange. Has LT a copyright on its own distinctive shade of red? The vehicle, of course, is again from the AEC stable and the bodyside route is a useful idea — though at the expense of lost advertising revenue. The date is 19 March 1994. Author

Above:
The mid-1970s saw LT facing an acute vehicle shortage and it was during this period that RT837 was pressed into service on route 28 seen here in Church Street, Kensington, the makeshift nature of the operation being shown by the mixture of RM and RT blinds.
V. H. Darling

Right:
28 January 1994 finds Dennis Dart DW113 on route 28. The unprepossessing frontage of Barclay's Bank has given way to a pizza parlour but otherwise the buildings are little changed. Unusually more 'To Let' signs are visible in the earlier shot than in the modern view.
Author

Right:
*RML2958 heads for the relief of
the bus lane as it passes Harrods
on route 14 on a short working to
Piccadilly Circus in March 1983.*
K. Lane

Above:
*Many aspects of London bus
operation were to change in the
ensuing 11 years but not all as
this view of RML2626 on the 14
exemplifies. Change, however,
has taken place in that the vehicle
has been fitted with an Iveco
engine and has been refurbished
as indicated by the different style
number plate. Oddly, at a time
when more bus lanes are
planned, this part of Brompton
Road has lost one — perhaps due
to the large number of taxis
which ply the area.*
Author

Above:
Acute vehicle shortage in 1948, LT's peak year for bus passengers carried, led to the newly-formed British Transport Commission ordering the diversion of 190

Tilling Group company vehicles of Bristol K-type with ECW, mostly lowbridge, bodies. All were returned by June 1950. Here is one of the visitors in Buckingham Palace Road helping out on route 11. V. C. Jones/IAL

Below:
RTL403 catches the sun nicely as it passes new office construction on the Albert Embankment on 18 June 1960. The offices were for the Metropolitan Police. The matching of registration numbers with fleet numbers really only began with the RMs though in some cases their now cherished registrations have passed to other vehicles. A. Hustwitt

Below left:
Today's route 11 terminates at Fulham Broadway rather than Shepherd's Bush and the destination is clearer on RML2363 than was the case with the lazy blinds fitted to the Bristol. The fluorescent lighting which forms part of the RML's refurbishment is visible on a dull 18 March 1994. Close inspection reveals that bomb damage to the upper floor of the library has been restored and the opportunity taken to add an additional room on the left.
Author

Above:
The 59A no longer exists and the 77 is one of only two routes to traverse the Albert Embankment, which is now widened so that traffic can screech to a halt at the Vauxhall interchange. All the old buildings on the far side of the road have disappeared under uninspired office blocks. Metrobus M589 displays its neat London General logo on 21 March 1994.
Author

Above:
Appropriately numbered RM1933 carries a version of London General livery to celebrate 50 years of LT and is seen in Camden High Street working route 24 on 6 October 1983. K. Lane

Below:
The take-over of route 24 by Grey Green heralded the penetration of independent tendered operation into Central London. Here Alexander-bodied Volvo Citybus No 140 is seen on 27 March 1994. The distinctive 'mens gear' premises seen in the previous view has been rebuilt. Author

Above:
The LT-type was unpopular with drivers on the 210 but survived until 1952, when the type was replaced in the short term by Qs demoted from Green Line work. LT1131 stands at the Wells Terrace (Finsbury Park) terminus whilst a TD, introduced to route 236 in 1948, stands in the background beneath the railway bridge leading to the coal yard. V. C. Jones/IAL

Below:
The Railway Hotel still stands but the background is much altered as Grey Green Volvo Citybus on route 120 enters Finsbury Park bus station on 16 August 1992. Author

Above:
One of the TDs seems to have strayed from the 236 and operates the 210 in Stroud Green Road at Finsbury Park. The driver's hand signals that he is slowing before turning into the terminus.
V. C. Jones/IAL

Below:
Some 40 years later and the background is remarkably little changed as RF672 participates in the Finsbury Park bus rally organised to celebrate the 40th anniversary of the Central Area RFs on 16 August 1992. RF672 was a Country Area example. Author

Top:
Still showing evidence of the recent conflict, with the first part of its name obliterated, the dilapidated Archway Tavern can witness every mode of LT road passenger transport as well as that of independent operators such as Birch Brothers whose Bristol K is seen on the busy junction. An LT-type operates route 210.
V. C. Jones/IAL

Above:
Inevitably, the Archway Tavern has become marooned in the middle of a one-way system. Independent operators are still in the picture but this time it is Grey Green providing LT service 210 on a tendered basis and its Volvo No 923 is seen on 5 April 1994. Author

Above:
This splendid view of Upper Street, Islington seems to have been taken from the top of a bus (or trolleybus) and is unusual in portraying all three types of LT road transport together. It depicts two STs, two STLs a borrowed Bristol, four 'E3'-type trams and a trolleybus ahead of the Bristol. The film Enchantment *advertised on the right of the picture was made in 1948.* V. C. Jones/IAL

Below:
Today's prospect depicts the triumph (?) of private transport. Taken on 18 February 1994 it shows two Metrobuses on rout 43 *and the distinctive rear of a Titan on route* 56. *The bus sto has been moved away from the junction which is probably where most passengers wanted to board or alight.*
Author

Above:
The photographer has secured an impressive view of RM1610 as it traverses a very wet Balls Pond Road in May 1984 working route 30.
Kevin Lane

Below:
Nearly 10 years later on 11 February 1994 route 30 is worked by T318 as it passes buildings little changed save for the shop frontages. Kan's Chinese takeaway boasts a new sign but is otherwise little altered. Author

Above:
RTL1534 enjoys the sunshine in Tollington Road, Holloway whilst working route 19 to Tooting Bec. The lack of people on the bus and only the young couple pushing a pram on the pavement suggest a quiet Sunday afternoon. Smokers may be able to date this 1960s shot more precisely from the advertisement for Cadets at 3s 6d (proper money!) for 20. V. C. Jones/IAL

Below:
A local resident had to identify the previous scene because it has now disappeared under a large Safeway's store. Though a Friday rather than a Sunday afternoon it is doubtful whether the unrelenting traffic would permit a clearer view of M630. The date is 11 February 1994.
Author

This picture:
RT3361 negotiates commercial vehicles unloading at will in Kilburn High Road in April 1961. A British Road Services' lorry follows the bus. The Magnificent Seven and Police Dog Story *are showing at the State cinema.*
W. H. R. Godwin

Right:
Probably the only reason Metrobus M618 is not having to negotiate parked vehicles is that Kilburn High Road is undergoing roadworks which have left an incredibly rough surface on February 1994. The State has sunk to a Bingo Hall and the bus stop has been resited. Author

Above:
Fortunately, the photographer provided full caption details for this shot of Metrobus M251 passing green RT3148 and red RT4028 which are returning from the RT Cavalcade of 5 April 1981. The buses are at Burnt Oak Broadway. Kevin Lane

Left:
The 79 no longer runs through Burnt Oak but BTS's Leyland Olympians on the 114 maintain a double-deck presence amongst a plethora of single-deck services. The weekday traffic circus that typifies most shopping centres is shown in this view on 29 March 1994. Author

Above:
G1, the first bus chassis to fit the Ministry of Supply's wartime specification, is seen leaving Golders Green bus station in the early 1950s. It carries a Park Royal body and was delivered in August 1942 but went straight into store because problems were experienced with the wartime version of the prewar Guy Arab chassis. It is setting out on the long 102 route to Chingford. The 'cleaner' smoking promised by the Craven A cork tips advertised on the side of the bus presages the smoking scare yet to come. V. C. Jones/IAL

Below:
On 27 March 1994 Metrobus M549 sets out on the last leg of its journey to Brent Cross. The other end of the route finishes at Edmonton. The Hippodrome still survives, like several other old London music halls, now in the ownership of the BBC. Author

Above:
M1479 illustrates a new departure for LT in that it was leased rather than owned outright. Twenty-nine of these MkII Metrobuses were leased for the Harrow Bus services from 1987–91 after which they were returned to dealers. M1479 stands above the M1 motorway at Hendon Midland station on route 183. M. Dryhurst

Left:
The 183 is now operated under the Metroline banner and by older Mk I Metrobuses, as represented by M1168 in this 25 March 1994 view. Author

Above:
A pleasant view of Metrobus M566 on route 221 in Alexandra Grove, Finchley, taken during April 1982. K. Lane

Right:
Twelve years later on 26 February 1994 little has changed though M1126 displays some minor differences such as the Leaside Buses insignia and the altered grille and headlight arrangement. The busy junctions behind the bus has gained a 'Give Way' sign but away from main roads change tends to be slower. Author

Above:
Initially there were 27 Country Area Cravens-bodied RTs of which RT1413 represents the type at New Barnet station on route 306 to Leavesden. The 120 distinctive Cravens bodies with their extra lower-deck window were the only bus bodies supplied by the firm to LT though it went on to provide Underground rolling stock. The Country Area Cravens were concentrated on Watford and Windsor garages and, being non-standard, were amongst the first RT withdrawals. Delivery of Cravens RTs was completed in 1950 and the attire of the waiting passengers and the cream upper-deck surrounds would suggest an early 1950s date for this view.
V. C. Jones/IAL

Above right:
The TF-type represented an important advance in single-decker design when the prototype appeared in 1937, as it could lay claim to being the first to be fitted with an engine designed for underfloor mounting. The objective, of course, was to provide greater seating capacity and the Green Line TF seated 34 passengers compared with the 30 of the 9T9-type introduced in 1936. By the date of this picture in 1949 TF86 had been relegated to Country Area work. It is seen at New Barnet station. V. C. Jones/IAL

Right:
Northern Counties-bodied Leyland Olympian No 57 of Atlas Bus works route 107 at New Barnet on 28 March 1994. The company has operated this route since 1989, its other LT-tendered service being the 112. The coal merchant's office has become a mini cab base, the attractive ironwork has disappeared and heavier traffic has necessitated a more disciplined approach to road marking in the station forecourt. Author

Right:
Enfield garage retained eight RTs to operate the 135 into 1978 but the 135A had been withdrawn by August 1977. Here an RT is seen in the attractive environment of Enfield Town.
P. J. Lynch

Below right:
Thamesway's Leyland-bodied Olympian No 1004 operates fendered route 307 to Brimsdown station, seen here on 5 April 1994. The shop fronts portray an updated image but all the major traders survive in a scene which shows surprisingly little change — other than in the volume of traffic.
Author

Below:
The ideal vehicle to complement Holden's distinctive station architecture at Southgate would be an RT but we have to make do with one of the neat Bristol LHs, BL80, seen loading for its run to Enfield on 20 April 1985, shortly before the route was taken over by Eastern National under tender. K. Lane

Above:
This modern view taken on 12 March 1994 reveals the continuing signs of recession with several empty shops and the circular sweep of the booking hall hidden behind hoardings — and the route boards on the bus shelter are still crooked! Eastern National's southern area has become Thamesway and is owned by the Badgerline group. Seen on the W9 is Mercedes Benz No 802 which carries Reeve Burgess Beaver bodywork. This bus seats 31, eight less than the Bristol. Author

Left:
Weyman-bodied Guy G422 is seen in Romford Road, Ilford on 1 June 1950 working route 86A which then ran from Upminster to Limehouse. The advertisement on the side is for National Savings which continued to be strongly promoted after the war.
R. E. Vincent

Below left:
The old premises of J. A. Symes are the only common feature to this 13 March 1994 view and the 1950 shot. Titan T470, unusually devoid of adverts, is glimpsed between the constant stream of traffic which now fills Romford Road. In 1950 the 86 ran between Chadwell Heath and Brentwood but today's 86 service from Romford to Stratford is the descendant of the erstwhile 86A.
Author

Top:
Looking handsome in its Green Line livery unmarred by advertisements, RT3258 is about to cross the River Roding as it leaves Ilford on route 721 on 25 August 1950. The advertisement for the locally-produced Ismay Lamps is interesting as is that for 'The World's Greatest Flying Display' at Farnborough. R. E. Vincent

Above:
The only common feature in this modern view is the Rose and Crown pub, the only other link with the past being the Keir Hardie Estate destination of T744 on route 147. The date is 13 March 1994.
Author

Left:
RM 1923 picks up in Chadwell Heath whilst working route 86 on 4 April 1982. K. Lane

Below:
Surviving Routemasters are mostly concentrated on Central London routes today and RM1923's replacement is T22. The stone bollards are presumably to prevent cars parking on the pavement. This shot could not be secured until a car parking on the bus stop in the road had moved! A new bus shelter and a new Sainsbury's supermarket are other changes from the earlier shot.
Author

Above:
Route 62's main claim to fame was that it was the last home of the classic RT — the last withdrawals from public service being on 7 April 1979. Four years later T141 is seen picking up outside The Brothers' Fish Bar in Station Road, Chadwell Heath on 24 May 1983. Author

Below:
By 1994 Dennis Darts, albeit the lengthened DRL version, are thought adequate to fulfil the 62's requirements . The date is 2 April. The fish bar and the opticians still survive — both perhaps fairly recession-proof businesses. Author

Above:
The then new Newbury Park bus station presents a striking image on 9 August 1949. The copper covered reinforced concrete barrel vault is 30ft high and 150ft long with an arched span of 60ft. An RT features in this fine illustration of LT's imaginative architectural work.
LTE

Below:
A somewhat less elegant prospect is presented in today's view taken on 2 April 1994 as Capital Citybus Leyland Olympian No 147 pauses briefly on route 296. The only other route to serve this stop is the 66, also operated by an independent, in this case County Bus.
Author

Above:
STL1780 and STL1243 are pictured on route 96 at Redbridge Central Line station bound for Putney Common on 23 May 1950. The first vehicle carries the handsome roofbox body introduced from 1936 whilst the second vehicle carries one of the 512 STL11-type bodies introduced in May 1935. R. E. Vincent

Below:
Many long cross-London routes have been pruned or withdrawn altogether, as was route 96 in 1958. The route number was reused on a southeast London route. Dennis Dart No 148 operates route 145 during a hailstorm on Easter Saturday 1994. Housing development has taken place since the previous picture and the distinctive lamp standards have disappeared. Author

Right:
Inroads were already being made on the Swift-type by the date of this photograph but SMS161 is fresh from an overhaul and has lost its Automatic Fare Collection (AFC) equipment as it picks up in Romford on route 248.
L. D. S. Nolan

Below:
2 April 1994 and route 248 is operated by Capital Citybus whose No 251 — a Northern Counties-bodied Dennis Dominator — picks up at stop 'Y' in Romford Station Parade. Douglas Allen has gone into partnership with Dennis Spiro and the Woolwich has usurped Kentons in the background.
Author

Above:
Brave New World (?). The newly opened Romford shopping centre with an SMS387 with coin in the slot symbols — but it looks very much as though the driver is taking fares. The date is 13 March 1971.
J. Rickard

Right:
Twenty-three years on it is 29 March 1994 and virtually nothing in the background has changed. Hunt & Hunt are still there (the legal profession seems fairly immune to economic cycles!) and none of the letters of the shopping centre sign have dropped off! But at least passengers on the 294 have been treated to a proper bus in the shape of T15.
Author

Above:
The advertisement carried on the side of TI may contravene the Trade Descriptions Act since the vehicle is in fact 10 years old in this 11 September 1988 view of the vehicle operating route 248 at Hornchurch White Hart. R. J. Waterhouse

Below:
The 248 is now operated by Capital Citybus and their No 261 is a Northern Counties-bodied Dennis Dominator. The Chinese lettering which forms part of the company logo featured on the side of the vehicle reflects the ownership of the operator by CNT, a Hong Kong-based group. Foreign involvement in the capital's transport is not new: French and American participation in bus and Underground operation dates from the turn of the century. Author

Above:
Unsuspecting passengers are subjected to the delights of SMS231 on the first day of one-person operation (one-man in the sexist days of 13 March 1971!). The bus is at the terminal point of route 252 in Low Shoe Lane, Colliers Row. J. Rickard

Right:
Today the 252 terminates rather more sensibly in the main shopping area and is another of the 26 main LT routes covered by Capital Citybus. No 126 is an Alexander-bodied Leyland Olympian and is seen on 2 April 1994 passing the end of Low Shoe Lane. Author

Above:
SMS409 works route 294 at Emerson Park on 27 March 1971, its exact fare requirement being another example of the reshaping plan vehicles' lack of passenger friendliness. V. C. Jones/IAL

Left:
*Today, the trees provide the main continuity from the earlier scene. Thameside's KPJ256W operates the 373 on 2 April 1994.
Author*

Above:
This pleasant view of T276 loading at the foot of King's Head Hill, Chingford on 25 October 1950 whilst operating route 205 conveys a relaxed atmosphere. T276 was one of a batch of 100 Green Line coaches dating from 1935. In 1938 it became one of the batch which received bus bodies which had originally been used to rebody AEC Reliance R-type vehicles. R. E. Vincent

Below:
The foot of King's Head Hill is far from peaceful today. Grey Green No 405, a Northern Counties-bodied Leyland Olympian, draws to a halt at the same stop on 5 April 1994. The financial services shop in the background and the private cars reflect the rise in affluence over the period.
Author

This picture:
An early 1960s shot at Clapham Common station and an RM on the 37. V. C. Jones/IAL

Inset:
The scene on 19 February 1994 shows relatively little change, though whilst the road signs have been modernised the LT roundel at the station has reverted to earlier style lettering. A refurbished RML works the 137. It is noticeable that increased traffic volumes has forced the resiting of the bus stop away from where passengers wish to go. Remarkably, Hazels survives as a hairdressers. Author

Above left:
The Sun at Clapham Old Town is the setting for handsome postwar STD129. Delivered in 1946 the STDs were based on Leyland's new PD1 chassis, its diesel engine being derived from one used in tanks during the war. STD129 was one of Victoria's allocation which it spread thinly over various routes before losing the postwar STDs to Stockwell in 1953.
V. C. Jones/IAL

Left:
STL582 rests at Clapham before commencing its long run to High Beach on route 35A. STL582 dates back to 1934. Perhaps the open-air telephone in use by the inspector inspired BT to inflict open call boxes on a later generation!
V. C. Jones/IAL

Above:
23 January 1994 finds route 137 still running to Oxford Circus, but in the hands of Iveco-engined RM348. The background buildings have recovered from the wartime neglect evident in the earlier views but the horse trough and the telephone are things of the past.
Author

Left:
Route 77B worked at weekends to Tooting during 1973 and the deserted nature of Lavender Hill suggests this is a Sunday working as RT3003 passes Arding & Hobbs.
V. C. Jones/IAL

Below:
30 January 1994 finds Metrobus 763 on route 77A whilst the sister vehicle behind on route 77 serves Tooting. The background is little changed except for the shops.
 Author

Above:
Omnia Transporters of Forest Hill was one of 159 operators to loan vehicles to LT during the period 1947–49 — but could this have been one of them? It carries no visible route number or LT insignia. In any case the STL in the background justifies the inclusion of this classic vehicle. 28 March 1948.
V. C. Jones/IAL

Below:
Utility Daimler D181 works route 88, its vertical radiator slats distinguishing its CWD6 chassis from the mesh type of the CWA6 which formed the majority of this final batch of 50 utility Daimlers delivered at the end of 1945. Carpenter's Confectioners displays some goodies to tempt customers beginning to be freed from rationing. The two roofbox STLs in the background display different widths of cream bands. V. C. Jones/IAL

Above:
Single-deck TF84's stylish lines date from 1939 though the prototype had been introduced two years earlier. The demountable route boards are reminiscent of railway practice and were perpetuated on the successor RFs whose underfloor engine was presaged by this advanced Leyland design. V. C. Jones/IAL

Below:
This April 1994 view is perhaps most remarkable for the continued existence of Arthur Knock and, less obviously, Evans who have wisely decided that 'The Outsize Shop' is not appropriate to this politically correct age. Metrobus M357 works route 37.
Author

Above:
A splendid collection of vehicles graces Clapham Common on 29 August 1948. STL 2183 on route 118 is one of a batch of Park Royal-bodied vehicles, delivery of which began in 1937. Behind it, STL 1167 carries one of a batch of 512 STL 11-type bodies and entered service in 1936. The summer weather has brought forth a rather natty pair of shorts on the gent on the right of the picture! Ian Allan Library

Below:
19 February 1994 shows remarkably little change in the surrounding buildings but private cars were much more in evidence and the bus scene is represented by Leyland Titan T 766 on route 45A and a pair of Metro buses on routes 319 and 37.
Author

Above:
'Balham — Gateway to the South' was a contemporary Peter Sellers' record parodying the dreadful travelogues which used to accompany main features at the cinema in the 1960s. An RTL passes on route 88.
V. C. Jones/IAL

Left:
Remarkably, Balham today is less of a 'Gateway to the South' — at least on buses. The five daytime routes which once served Balham High Road being reduced to two and the road no longer sees double-deck vehicles. A Dennis Dart represents the current scene on 19 February 1994. The pedestrian crossing is now traffic-light controlled, a new office block has appeared near the station and the concrete lamp-posts have been replaced. Otherwise little else has changed. Author

Above:
In an atmosphere reminiscent of the contemporary film Up the Junction, RT1659 turns into Denmark Hill at Camberwell whilst working route 45 in the early 1960s. V. C. Jones/IAL

Below:
Hoardings around a building site prevented the same angle being obtained on 5 February 1994. Leyland Titan T970 performs the same manoeuvre. The background buildings have been smartened up but surprisingly the lamp standards look the same as the originals. Author

Above:
'Feltham' tram No 2090 seen in Mitcham Lane operating route 10 to Tooting Broadway and passing some classic period shops on 14 October 1950 was too good to miss. The pram and the tricycle are other vintage vehicles. Ian Allan Library

Below:
Dennis Dart DRL152 passes the same spot on 19 February 1994. The newsagent has diversified into food, The Buffet has become a Chinese takeaway and whilst kebabs are the main offering, fish and chips are still available on the site of the old Friary Fish Restaurant. Author

Above:
This 1970s view of Tooting Broadway shows RM353 on route 64 and an RT on route 19, neither of which now run as far as Tooting, the former terminating at Thornton Heath and the latter at Battersea.
Ian Allan Library

Below:
Other than the lamp-posts, the surroundings display remarkably little change by 26 February 1994 as Metrobus M970 heads for Battersea on the 219, providing a link with the current route 19. The lack of rear destination display is characteristic of rear-engined buses. Author

Above:
Some splendid vehicles in this 1960s shot of RM1348 working route 37 in Wandsworth's York Road.
V. C. Jones/IAL

Below:
Metrobus M842 traverses the eastbound one-way street at this altered junction on 26 February 1994 whilst operating route 37. Author

Above:
Daimler D208 works route 93 in Putney High Street. The vehicle was one of a postwar batch of 100 Daimlers delivered from 1946 and allocated to Sutton garage throughout their lives. The body was by Park Royal to 'relaxed austerity' standard. The three-part destination box is not fully utilised. It is the days when 'Wisk' had an amazing new formula and men weren't dragged around shops.
V. C. Jones/IAL

Right:
Route 93 still runs to the same terminal point in North Cheam, which is the destination of Metrobus M1220 on 19 March 1994. Like its predecessor the full destination panel is not utilised and advertising space is reduced. Other than having been cleaned up the background buildings show little change. Author

Above:
RT2527 enjoys an unimpeded passage along Streatham High Road as tram tracks are removed. No marks for the architect responsible for the blocks of flats. Ian Allan Library

Below:
It is 26 March 1994 and the scene looks as though it may have been taken by a group advocating restoration of trams or light rapid transport in today's jargon. An RM in special livery for route 159 contends with the traffic. The white window frames make the flats look slightly less forbidding but they have somewhat inexplicably sprouted extra chimneys. Author

This picture:
Route 37 is a long established route which plied between Hounslow and Peckham as shown by the ultimate destinations on the two RMs shown in this 1960s view of Herne Hill. This was a period of relative calm in LT operations with trolleybus replacement completed in 1962 and before the reshaping scheme was unleashed in 1968. V. C. Jones/IAL

Below:
Leyland Titan T760 operates route 40 at the same location on 19 February 1994. The gap between the buildings has been filled-in by new premises and the advertising hoardings on the railway bridge have disappeared. The eastbound bus stop has gained a shelter and whilst the newsagent and tobacconist survives, Steve's Cafe has become a firm of solicitors. Yellow lines have made their appearance, apparently with little effect! Author

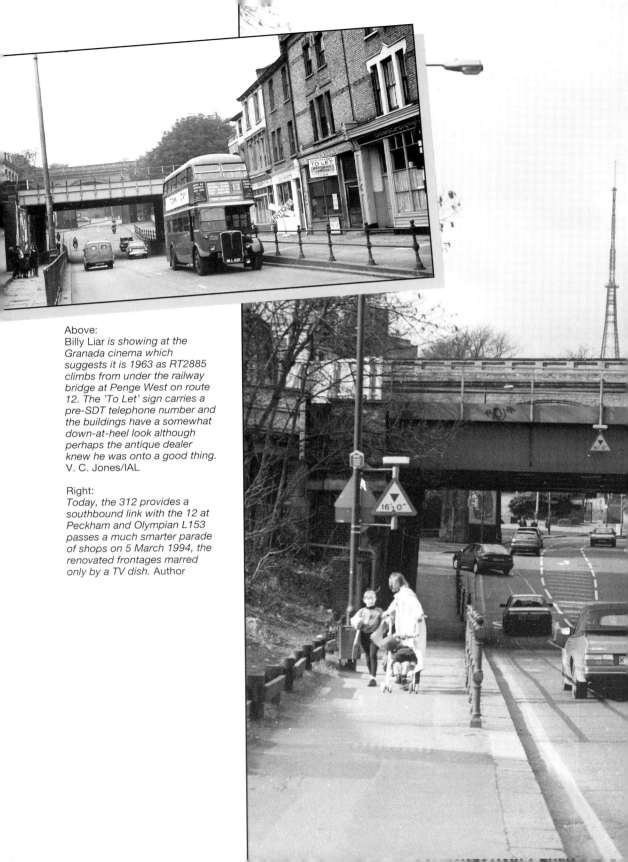

Above:
Billy Liar *is showing at the Granada cinema which suggests it is 1963 as RT2885 climbs from under the railway bridge at Penge West on route 12. The 'To Let' sign carries a pre-SDT telephone number and the buildings have a somewhat down-at-heel look although perhaps the antique dealer knew he was onto a good thing.* V. C. Jones/IAL

Right:
Today, the 312 provides a southbound link with the 12 at Peckham and Olympian L153 passes a much smarter parade of shops on 5 March 1994, the renovated frontages marred only by a TV dish. Author

Above left:
An RT climbs out of the drab surroundings of Norwood Junction on route 75 during the 1960s. The crane in the background starts work on the flats which appear in the next pictures. V. C. Jones/IAL

Above:
Leyland Titan T1076 looks more sprightly in the sunshine of 26 February 1994. Gipsy Hill Car Dismantlers has become David House but perhaps the adjacent Dukie's Car Parts is a descendant. The Waldocks Newsagent sign is still on the side of the building. Author

Left:
As various other pictures illustrate it was not unusual to see different types on one route in the early 1950s but as standardisation spread it became uncommon. The greater choice of vehicle types since then has enabled operators to match vehicle capacity (and costs) to likely demand though the Dennis Lance LA7 was initially introduced onto Catford's route 36B to overcome problems to top deck vandalism. The date is 26 February 1994. Author

Above:
An interesting collection of vehicles at the old West Croydon bus station on 11 September 1971 with London Country's SM533 and RT3173 and LT's DMS139 and XA31. The latter is on route C4 — an early example of area prefix letters being applied to the route numbers.
S. J. A. Madden

Left:
Metrobus M1104 working route 403 provides a tenuous link with the earlier picture. By 5 February 1994 the bus station has been rebuilt. It still seems strange to see red buses working routes in the 400 series. Author

Right:
Morden station was a favourite location for early bus photographs, forming an important underground railhead for the expanding south London suburbs from which seven routes departed in 1938 to serve the surrounding area. Merton and Sutton garages were the homes to the Daimler CW buses of the D-type. DI with utility Duple lowbridge bodywork entered service in 1944 and is seen in postwar years on route 127. The last Daimlers were withdrawn from service in early 1954 but many saw service elsewhere including Belfast, Southend and Colombo. In rebodied form some lasted into the 1960s.
V. C. Jones/IAL

Above:
Buses now stop facing the opposite direction and a rather more prosaic (though rather more comfortable) Metrobus illustrates the scene on 5 March 1994. Despite altered traffic patterns six routes still serve the terminus today of which the 80 can trace its roots back to prewar days. Frequencies, however, are somewhat reduced and the diminished significance of the station is emphasised by the encroaching office blocks. One looks in vain for Air France advertising flights to Paris for £10! Author

101

Above:
T-type T745 works route 213 at the Fountain Hotel, New Malden in the early 1950s, the puddle under the bus shelter demonstrating the ineffectiveness of the structure. This bus was one of a batch of Weymann-bodied Ts delivered in 1946. They were the first type of London motor bus to be fitted with horizontally sliding windows. V. C. Jones/IAL

Below:
The bus stop has been resited slightly by 12 March 1994 as Metrobus M662 draws up on the 213 which now does not run beyond Sutton. The newsagent survives with a new front and abbreviated blind but permanent waving is no longer offered. The Fountain Hotel still functions but the trolleybus poles are a thing of the past. Author

Right:
Alexander-bodied Mercedes Benz 811D MA37 operates route 28 in West End Lane, Kilburn on 11 March 1989. The conversion of this route from full-size vehicles to minibuses did not meet with universal approval amongst its patrons who may have felt the closeness of its brand name to that of the luxury rail service merely added insult to injury. K. Lane

Below:
At first sight the Dennis Dart seems a step up for passengers on the 28 though surprisingly its Wright Handybus body in fact seats two fewer passengers than the mini bus and its standing capacity of five more may not exactly endear it to them. The Northern Ireland registration, deriving from the Belfast home of its bodybuilder, sits oddly on a London bus. The date is 19 March 1994. Author

Above:
This veteran, LT1677, of a type introduced by the London General Omnibus Co in 1929, contrasts with one of the new RTs which will soon condemn prewar types to oblivion in this view outside Shepherd's Bush garage in the late 1940s. V. C. Jones/IAL

Left:
The garage has been rebuilt, though surprisingly the cobbles remain as refurbished RML2349 runs-in off route 94 on 16 April 1994. Author

Above:
The opening of the Hammersmith flyover entailed major road works in the surrounding area including the construction of Butterwick bus station which opened in mid-1958 and originally played host to trolleybuses as well as diesel buses. The withdrawal of the trolleybuses encouraged a smartening up of the facilities in the early 1960s and this photograph shows them off well. RF135 picks up on route 716A. LTE

Below:
16 January 1994 finds the Butterwick facilities standing idle as Plaxton Pointer-bodied Dennis Dart DR102 heads for the new Hammersmith bus station whose opening the previous year led to the redundancy of the Butterwick facilities.
Author

The new Hammersmith bus station provides far better passenger facilities than did Butterwick and this view is taken from inside the fully-enclosed waiting area. Refurbished RML2295 operates route 10 on 16 January 1994. Author

Right:
19 January 1994 saw Armchair operation of route 65 enter its third year. Under this operator the now truncated route continues to see a variety of vehicle types - in this case a 1991 Leyland Olympian. Author

Below:
Adding to the variety at Ealing Broadway was one of the lowbridge Bristols diverted from their originally intended recipients by the BTC to relieve LT's vehicle shortage. It is operating route 97. V. C. Jones/IAL

Above left:
B6, one of 10 'unfrozen' Bristol K5Gs, was delivered to Hanwell in May 1942 for service on route 97. 'Unfrozen' buses were those which were allowed to be built to prewar specifications. Whilst always associated with the 97 they also worked routes 18C, 55, 83/A and 92/A. V. C. Jones/IAL

Left:
TD103 on route 211: a Leyland Tiger PS1 with a Mann Egerton body, it was delivered to Hanwell in 1949 and its gleaming paintwork suggests it has only just arrived. V. C. Jones/IAL

Above:
Now a plethora of E-prefixed routes serve Ealing Broadway, operated by Wright-bodied Renault 50s of the RW class. RW14 waits to resume service on the E2 on 9 January 1994.
Author

Right:
RM476 entered service in November 1960 and by November 1963 official policy had decreed that offside route numbers should no longer be displayed. Since this is an official AEC picture it is likely to be nearer the start of that period than the end. The Iron Bridge at Southall proudly points the way to the birthplace of the bus.
AEC

Above:
2 January 1994 shows no evidence of AEC remaining. The 207 is operated by MCW Metrobus M1201 and the site of the famous works is now an industrial park. A separate filter lane for Windmill Lane has been built. Author

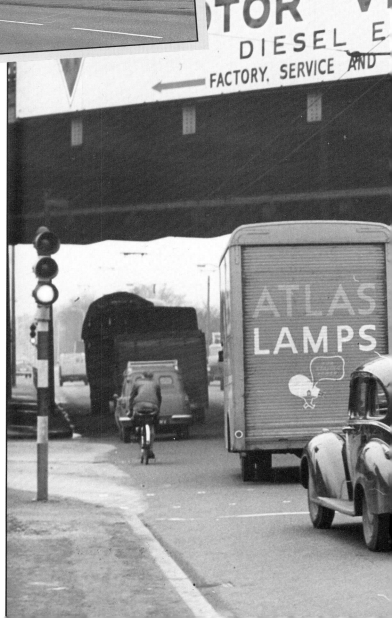

Above:
M495 seen in Uxbridge Road, West Ealing on 2 March 1981 illustrates the vicissitudes through which the Ealing-based routes have passed since 1968. Originally an MBS-operated route it had graduated to double-deckers by the date of this picture but still operated on a flat fare. Author

Left:
2 January 1994 and the E1 no longer services Uxbridge Road but, like the E3 shown here, it is operated by a Renault 50 minibus with Wright bodywork — hence the Irish registrations. The vehicle is RW16. Author

Above:
*The famous 'Meccano Set'
STL2477 to which a unique new
body built in the experimental
section of Chiswick works was
fitted in 1950. Officially known as
the Sainsbury body, after its
designer, the idea was to allow
quick and easy replacement of
the bolt-on body panels and
components. The bus was
withdrawn from LT service in
1954 but it lasted until 1958 in
service with Bee Line, West
Hartlepool.* V. C. Jones/IAL

Right:
*Despite appearances to the
contrary, London Buslines' No 49,
an Alexander-bodied Olympian, is
actually working route 79 on
which G75 is working in the
previous shot. This time route 83
worked by M465 plays second
fiddle. The background offices
have been rebuilt. The date is
16 April 1994.* Author

115

Above left:
Myrna Loy appeared in the film Cheaper by the Dozen *in 1950 and this dates this view in another of the bus photographers' erstwhile favourite locations, Cromwell Road, Kingston. T207 was a 1930s 1/7T7/1 originally built for Green Line work. Route 218 crossed a weak bridge at Walton and thus prolonged the life of some of the lightweight early Ts. The bridge was strengthened in 1953.* F. G. Reynolds

Above:
T536 in the same location: its Chiswick-built body bearing little resemblance to that of T207 and reminding one that particularly within the T and STL classes great visual variety could be found. TDs arrived to replace 10T10s such as T536 in 1953 so the newer road surface compared to the previous view would suggest a date between 1950 and 1953. V. C. Jones/IAL

Left:
Today, Cromwell Road is one way heading south. London and Country's SNB440 waits in the sunshine on 26 March 1994. Though the railway still runs in the background no trace is visible. Buses stand in the old goods yard which has lost its fence of railway sleepers. Author

Above:
Tarzan's New York Adventure *was made in 1942 but the accompanying Olympic Preview at the quaintly named Kinema suggests the date is 1948 as T310 leaves Kingston Bus Station on a 213 to Belmont. The Kingston area has a long association with single-deck routes. V. C. Jones/IAL*

Below:
All buses must now turn right into the inevitable one-way system to which Kingston appears to have been largely given over. Metrorider MR52 brings up the rear of a convoy of buses seeking a gap in the traffic. The Kinema has become Pine World and the Rickett & Cockerill Coal and Coke Office has disappeared under an office block. The date is 19 March 1994. Author

Above:
Again the cinema comes to the rescue: Q26 was built in 1935 with a Country Area central doorway body. Its side mounted engine was a great advance on contemporary single-deck vehicles and permitted a significant increase in capacity. Dulcie Gray appeared in My Brother Jonathan *in 1949 which thus dates this view taken outside the Elite cinema in Kingston where three cinemas could be found at that time within about 1/4 mile. V. C. Jones/IAL*

Below:
The Elite cinema became C&A's—at least avoiding the indignity of conversion into a bingo hall. A Metrorider negotiates the one-way system on 19 March 1994. Author

Above:
A Leyland MkI National battles through traffic in Kingston on 27 August 1980. Author

Left:
The view on 26 March 1994 shows that the street has been pedestrianised. It would seem to be a fairly unique example of such schemes for no delivery vehicles or cars carrying disabled stickers are to be seen! Author

Above:
BL20 displaying an attractive livery with cream window surrounds picks up in Kingston on route 201 in March 1979. K. Lane

Below:
MR30, an MCW Metrorider, in surroundings little changed from the 1979 view, represents something of an anomaly with respect to route numbering. Route 501 is a Surrey County Council tendered service running between Kingston Hospital and Esher and is the only example of the same number being used for two different services — the other 501 being a Red Arrow route between Waterloo and London Bridge stations. Fortunately, this black and white view masks the full horror of the Westlink livery! The date is 26 March 1994. Author

Above:
A peaceful summer scene at Teddington in the 1960s with an RM on route 281.
V. C. Jones/IAL

Left:
Kingston was a pleasant riverside town until it was abandoned to the motor car. Now traffic starts queuing on the other side of the bridge in Teddington to gain access to its car parks. This February 1994 shot shows M836 on route 281. Unusually, the Do It Yourself store has been converted to a private dwelling.
Author

Above:
The new bus station facilities at Hounslow nearing completion in 1969 play host to two classic vehicle types — the RT and RF with a Merlin MBS as the interloper. Ten MBS were fitted with modified automatic fare collecting equipment to operate routes 110 and 111. V. C. Jones/IAL

Below:
The bus station has worn quite well over the intervening 25 years and in this 5 April 1994 view a Dennis Dart, a Metrobus, one of nine Optare Delta-bodied DAFs delivered in 1989/90 and used on tendered route 110, and a London Buslines' Leyland Lynx show a range of successors. Author

Above:
The Leyland National was to prove a rather more durable successor to the ill-fated Swift vehicles which had introduced one man operation to route 111. LS47 loads outside Hounslow bus station. M. Curtis

Below:
The 111 has reverted to double-deck operation and Metrobus M1238 does the honours on 5 April 1994. The Duke of Cambridge shows little change in the background. Author

Above:
Low bridges have been a source of problems to LT. Route 230 had been worked by single-deck vehicles of the Q class at the start of the war. October 1942 saw increased passenger demands lead to the introduction of lowbridge STLs. STL1978 seen at Harrow & Wealdstone in the early 1950s shows the lowbridge body which it acquired in 1941. V. C. Jones/IAL

Below:
Route 230 became H1 in 1969 and reverted to single-deck operation. Today the H10 covers the route and is in the hands of Sovereign whose Reeve Burgess Beaver-bodied Mercedes Benz 811D No 421 is seen on 29 March 1994. Bunting continues to sell cycles but the splendid television showroom has become a jewellers. Author

Above:
STL2232 is another wartime lowbridge conversion. It is seen at Rayners Lane with Peter's pet shop in the background. V. C. Jones/IAL

Below:
Surprisingly the pet shop still exists though slightly relocated in a block whose architectural style echoes that of LT's Underground station on the other side of the road. Was Mr Holden moonlighting? Sovereign's No 424 is seen on 12 March 1994. Author

Above:
Such was the shortage of lowbridge vehicles that six vintage National/Amersham STs were fitted with oil engines from STLs in 1949 to enable them to soldier on for two years after their conventional sisters had been withdrawn in 1950. ST141 is in Harrow after its allocation to Harrow Weald in July 1951. V. C. Jones/IAL

Below:
The distinctive gable ends in Masons Avenue survive as Sovereign's K5 SBC fitted with smart card equipment draws up at another resited stop on 29 March 1994. Author

Top:
The Weymann-bodied RLHs were diverted from a Midland General order by direction of the British Transport Commission, putting paid to a putative lowbridge version of the RM. The first were delivered in 1950 but Harrow Weald only received an allocation from the second batch at the end of 1952. RLH 64 is seen in Kenton Road. V. C. Jones/IAL

Above:
The H10 runs along Kenton Road but it was felt that some people might feel that a fourth shot of a Sovereign minibus was a bit too much of a good thing! So BTS's L141, a Northern Counties-bodied Leyland Olympian, is shown at this location instead. The date is 29 March 1994. Author